SPORTS
VIPs

MEET
ALLYSON FELIX

MATT DOEDEN

Lerner Publications ◆ Minneapolis

SPORTS THRILLS *MEET* RESEARCH SKILLS

Lerner SPORTS

Free Database Trial: **lernersports.com**

Lerner Publications Company
An imprint of Lerner Publishing Group, Inc.
241 First Avenue North
Minneapolis, MN 55401 USA

For reading levels and more information, look up this title at www.lernerbooks.com.

Main body text set in Aptifer Slab LT Pro. Typeface provided by Linotype AG.

Designer: Kim Morales

Library of Congress Cataloging-in-Publication Data

Names: Doeden, Matt, author.
Title: Meet Allyson Felix / Matt Doeden.
Description: Minneapolis, MN : Lerner Publications, [2023] | Series: Sports VIPS (Lerner Sports) | Includes
    bibliographical references and index. | Audience: Ages 7–11 years | Audience: Grades 2–3 | Summary: "US
    track-and-field superstar Allyson Felix competed in five Olympic Games. In 2021, Felix won her 11th Olympic
    track-and-field medal, more than any other athlete in US history. Explore her life on and off the track"—
    Provided by publisher.
Identifiers: LCCN 2021054010 (print) | LCCN 2021054011 (ebook) | ISBN 9781728458199 (Library Binding) |
    ISBN 9781728463292 (Paperback) | ISBN 9781728462271 (eBook)
Subjects: LCSH: Felix, Allyson, 1985– —Juvenile literature. | Women track and field athletes—United States—
    Biography—Juvenile literature. | Track and field athletes—United States—Biography—Juvenile literature. |
    African American athletes—Biography—Juvenile literature. | Women Olympic athletes—United States—
    Biography—Juvenile literature. | University of Southern California—Alumni and alumnae.
Classification: LCC GV697.F45 D63 2023 (print) | LCC GV697.F45 (ebook) | DDC 796.42092 [B]—dc23/eng/20211122

LC record available at https://lccn.loc.gov/2021054010
LC ebook record available at https://lccn.loc.gov/2021054011

Manufactured in the United States of America
1-50849-50186-2/21/2022

TABLE OF CONTENTS

>>>>>>>>>>>>>>>>>>>>>>

CHASING HISTORY

Allyson Felix needed to run during summer 2020. The Olympic Games that year had been postponed. The deadly illness COVID-19 was sweeping around the world. Her normal gyms and training centers shut down to avoid spreading the disease.

"It was something that was really hard to deal with," Felix said. "As an Olympic athlete, timing is everything, and you make so many sacrifices to be able to be ready in the moment. So when I learned that it wasn't going to be happening, it was pretty crushing."

FAST FACTS

DATE OF BIRTH: November 18, 1985
POSITION: sprinter
LEAGUE: USA Track and Field

PROFESSIONAL HIGHLIGHTS: was the *Track and Field News* 2003 High School Athlete of the Year; is an 11-time Olympic medalist (seven gold, three silver, and one bronze); won 12 world championships

PERSONAL HIGHLIGHTS: grew up in Los Angeles, California; graduated from the University of Southern California (USC) with a degree in elementary education; married Kenneth Ferguson and welcomed daughter Camryn in 2018

Felix (*left*) turns on the speed during the women's 400-meter final at the Olympic Games in 2021.

Felix didn't let the canceled Olympics stop her from training. She ran around her neighborhood in Los Angeles. She ran at empty soccer fields, baseball fields, and beaches.

Felix's hard work paid off. In August 2021, the Olympics were back on. Felix headed to Tokyo, Japan, with the US track-and-field team. She was chasing history. Felix had already won nine Olympic medals in her career. One more would give her the most in the history of women's track and field at the Olympics.

Felix earned a spot in the 400-meter final. But a medal seemed unlikely. She had the second-slowest time to qualify for the race. At 35, she was older than most other Olympic athletes. And she got off to a terrible start in the final. But Felix dug deep. In the last 100 meters, she surged forward. She passed runner after runner and crossed the finish line in third place. She'd won the bronze medal—the 10th medal of her amazing career.

Felix holds her 400-meter bronze medal. All of her other Olympic medals are gold or silver.

CHAPTER 1

BORN TO RUN

Allyson Felix was born on November 18, 1985, in Los Angeles, California. Her mom, Marlean, was a teacher. Her dad, Paul, was a minister. Allyson grew up in Los Angeles with her older brother, Wes. No one in the family called Allyson by her name. They called her Shug instead. The nickname was short for *sugar*.

Wes and Allyson were both good athletes. They shared a passion for sports. Allyson cheered on Wes as he became a top amateur sprinter. She made up her mind to follow in his footsteps.

Wes Felix (*left*) and Allyson Felix (*right*) in 2004. Wes later became a sports agent and helped Allyson and other track-and-field athletes with business deals.

Allyson attended Los Angeles Baptist High School in North Hills, California. She dreamed of being a basketball player or a gymnast. She said that playing sports helped shape her. "[Sports] gave me confidence, taught me work ethic, leadership, how to deal with failure, the value of teamwork and countless other invaluable lessons I still rely on today," she wrote.

Allyson waves to the crowd after winning a race for Los Angeles Baptist High School.

Allyson's smooth running style and long strides helped her zoom around the track.

In 2000, her focus shifted to running. As a ninth grader, she made the school's track-and-field team. It didn't take Allyson long to make a big impact for the team. She took home seventh place in the 200-meter race at the California State Meet.

Allyson runs for Team USA in 2001.

Allyson quickly became a rising track-and-field star. In 2001, she won first place in the 100-meter race at the World Youth Championships in Debrecen, Hungary.

Allyson kept winning races. *Track and Field News* named her the 2003 girls High School Athlete of the Year. One of her biggest moments that year came at a meet in Mexico City, Mexico. Allyson blazed to victory in the 200-meter with a time of 22.11 seconds. It would have been a junior world record. But the time didn't count because the event did not meet all the rules for official records.

SUPER SPORTS SCOOP

Like many sports, track and field has problems with athletes using performance-enhancing drugs (PEDs). PEDs can give athletes an advantage on the track. But PEDs also put their health at risk. Felix volunteers for Project Believe. She goes through extra testing to show everyone she can win without PEDs.

CHAPTER 2

GOING PRO

After graduating from high school in 2003, Felix planned to join the track-and-field team at USC. But her amazing 200-meter time in Mexico City changed her plans. She decided to turn pro instead. Felix signed an endorsement deal with the shoe company Adidas. As part of the deal, Adidas agreed to pay for her education at USC. She went on to graduate with a degree in elementary education

Meanwhile, Felix continued to train and compete. At the 2003 US national championships, she finished second in the 200-meter race.

Felix accepts her trophy after becoming the 2002–2003 Gatorade National Girls Track-and-Field Athlete of the Year.

SUPER SPORTS SCOOP

Success isn't easy for Felix. She trains for about five hours each day. She spends about three hours on the track stretching, doing exercises, and running. The other two hours are in the gym. She works on strengthening her muscles, heart, and lungs.

At 18, Felix earned a spot on the 2004 US Olympic team. She traveled to Athens, Greece, with the team in August to compete in the 200-meter. In the final, Felix didn't get off to a great start. Jamaica's Veronica Campbell-Brown gained a big lead. Felix turned on the speed late in the race. She closed the gap to Campbell-Brown, but she could not catch her. Felix finished second to earn the silver medal. It was the first medal of her Olympic career.

Felix kept getting better. In 2005, she won the 200-meter race at the world championships. At 19, she was the youngest world champion ever in the event. Two years later, she defended her title with her fastest time to date at 21.81 seconds.

Felix won the 200-meter race at the 2007 world championships by 0.53 seconds. No one had won the race by such a large margin in 59 years.

CHAPTER 3

BUILDING A LEGACY

As the 2008 Olympics in Beijing, China, approached, Felix was preparing to do more than just the 200-meter. She also trained for the 100-meter race and two relay events. She failed to qualify for the 100-meter. But she made the team for both the 200-meter and 4 x 400-meter relays.

Felix's Olympics started out with a disappointment. In the 200-meter final, she lost a tight race to Campbell-Brown. Felix finished second to take silver. But the US team blazed to victory in the 4 x 400. Felix stood proudly at the top of the medal stand with her teammates.

Left to right: Mary Wineberg, Allyson Felix, Monique Henderson, and Sanya Richards-Ross show off their gold medals after the women's 4 x 400-meter relay at the 2008 Olympic Games.

SUPER SPORTS SCOOP

What does a gold-medal diet look like? Here's a typical day of food for Felix:

Breakfast—yogurt and granola
Mid-morning snack—smoothie
Lunch—salad with fruit and meat, such as chicken
Dinner—fish, brown rice, and vegetables

Felix was becoming one of the biggest stars in track and field. But she still wanted more. At the 2012 Olympics in London, England, she competed in four events. It made for a busy schedule. But she was ready.

Felix finished fifth in the 100-meter race and didn't earn a medal. But she made up for it with her other three events. She used a strong start to win gold in the 200-meter. Next came the 4 x 100-meter relay. Felix and her teammates dominated. They earned gold with a world-record time of 40.82 seconds. Then Felix finished with a gold medal in the 4 x 400-meter relay. Three gold medals! Felix was on top of the track-and-field world.

A leg injury slowed Felix down in 2013 and 2014. But she was back on the track for the 2015 world championships. She won gold in the 400-meter race.

Felix brought her three gold medals from the London Olympics to the Empire State Building in New York City for a photo shoot on August 15, 2012.

Shaunae Miller (*bottom*) reaches across the finish line just ahead of Felix (*top*) in the 400-meter final.

The victory gave Felix confidence for the 2016 Olympics in Rio de Janeiro, Brazil. An ankle injury prevented her from qualifying for the 200-meter. But she was in the middle of a thrilling 400-meter final. Felix streaked to the finish line. It looked as if she would win. But Shaunae Miller of the Bahamas dove across the line in the final moment to beat Felix by 0.07 seconds.

The 4 x 100-meter relay almost ended in disaster. Felix dropped the baton. At first, the US team was disqualified. But replays showed that another runner had bumped into Felix. The US team was allowed to continue. They went on to win gold in the final. Felix added another gold in the 4 x 400-meter relay. That gave her nine career Olympic medals, tying Merlene Ottey of Jamaica for the most ever in women's track and field.

The baton falls between Felix (*right*) and English Gardner (*left*) during the 4 x 100-meter relay. A Brazilian runner had bumped into Felix, causing her to miss the handoff to Gardner.

CHAPTER 4

GOLD-MEDAL MOM

Felix's life changed in 2018. She married fellow runner Kenneth Ferguson. Felix had to take a break from competing for a good reason—she was pregnant with her first child.

Being pregnant wasn't easy for Felix. Doctors discovered she had a condition that caused her to have high blood pressure. It put the baby at risk. So doctors performed an emergency operation to safely deliver the baby.

"It's amazing how quickly your priorities change in moments like this," Felix wrote on Twitter. "At that point, the only thing I cared about was that my daughter, Camryn, was OK. I didn't care if I ever ran track again."

Felix and her daughter have fun on the track at the 2020 US Olympic Team Trials.

Felix runs at the Tokyo Olympics in 2021.

Pregnancy and the surgery were hard on Felix. She didn't compete for more than a year. She spent time fighting for the rights of pregnant athletes. Felix wanted athletes to continue to receive money from endorsements even when they couldn't compete because of pregnancy.

Felix knew that at 35, the 2021 Olympics would be her last. But she was eager to show her daughter that with hard work, anything was possible.

After taking bronze in the 400-meter, Felix prepared for her last event, the 4 x 400-meter relay. The US team ran away from the others. They won by almost four seconds to earn gold. Felix had her 11th Olympic medal. That was more than any other US track-and-field athlete in history.

Felix said she doesn't plan to return to the Olympics in 2024. But that doesn't mean her career is over. She hasn't ruled out competing at the 2022 world championships. Can she win another medal at 36? After her amazing career, it's tough to count her out.

SUPER SPORTS SCOOP

What will Felix do when her running career is over? She thinks she might become a teacher. She loves kids and could use her college degree in elementary education. How cool would it be to have a world champion as your teacher?

ALLYSON FELIX CAREER STATS

OLYMPIC GAMES:

5

(2004, 2008, 2012, 2016, 2021)

100-METER FASTEST TIME:

10.89

SECONDS

OLYMPIC MEDALS:

11

(7 GOLD, 3 SILVER, 1 BRONZE)

200-METER FASTEST TIME:

21.69

SECONDS

WORLD CHAMPIONSHIPS:

12

400-METER FASTEST TIME:

49.26

SECONDS

Stats are accurate through November 1, 2021.

GLOSSARY

amateur: an athlete who is not paid to compete in a sport

baton: a stick that relay runners pass from one runner to the next

endorsement: when someone recommends a product, usually in exchange for money

final: the last race in a track-and-field event

meet: a competition that includes a variety of track-and-field events

pro: short for professional, an athlete who competes in a sport to earn money

qualify: to run fast enough in a race to take part in the final

relay: a race between teams in which each team member covers a certain part of the track

smoothie: a creamy drink made of fruit blended with juice, milk, or yogurt

sprinter: an athlete who competes in short, fast running events

SOURCE NOTES

5 Nicholas Rice, "Allyson Felix Says the Pandemic Forced Her to 'Get Creative' about Training for the Olympics," People.com, December 18, 2020, https://people.com/sports/allyson-felix-olympics-training-exclusive/.

10 Nick McCarvel, "Allyson Felix: Five Things You Don't Know," Olympics.com, February 8, 2021, https://olympics.com/en/news/allyson-felix-five-things-mum-camryn-basketball.

25 Allyson Felix (@allysonfelix), Twitter, December 20, 2018, https://twitter.com/allysonfelix/status/1075780850581757952.

LEARN MORE

Gitlin, Marty. *Olympic Track and Field Legends*. Mankato, MN: Bolt, 2021.

Levit, Joseph. *Track and Field's G.O.A.T.: Usain Bolt, Jackie Joyner-Kersee, and More*. Minneapolis: Lerner Publications, 2022.

McDonald, Scott. *Record Breakers*. Philadelphia: Mason Crest, 2020.

Olympic Games
https://olympics.com/en

Team USA—Allyson Felix
https://www.teamusa.org/usa-track-and-field/athletes/allyson-felix

USA Track and Field
https://www.usatf.org/

INDEX

PHOTO ACKNOWLEDGMENTS

Image credits: Felix Sanchez Arrazola/Alamy Stock Photo, p. 4; Christian Petersen/Getty Images, pp. 6, 26; Tim Clayton/Corbis via Getty Images, p. 7; Kirby Lee/WireImage/Getty Images, pp. 8, 10, 12; Kirby Lee via AP, pp. 9, 11; Matthew Stockman/Getty Images, p. 14; AP Photo/Matt Sayles, p. 15; Gouhier-Kempinaire/Cameleon/Abaca Press/Alamy Stock Photo, p. 17; GABRIEL BOUYS/AFP via Getty Images, p. 18; AP Photo/Petr David Josek, p. 19; AP Photo/Alex Katz, p. 21; Kyodo via AP Images, p. 22; FRANCK FIFE/AFP via Getty Images, p. 23; David Ramos/Getty Images, p. 24; Steph Chambers/Getty Images, p. 25. Design elements: The Hornbills Studio/Shutterstock.com; Tamjaii9/Shutterstock.com.

Cover: REUTERS/Aleksandra Szmigiel/Alamy Stock Photo.